First Book of VERBS

An Early Language Book

Cara Tambellini Danielson M.A. CCC-SLP

Illustrator: Mary Tambellini

Note from the author:

I love teaching children verbs. Once they have verbs in their vocabulary, they can start to combine them with nouns to form phrases and sentences. All of the sentences in this book follow the same basic structure – noun + is + verb-ing. This is a great starting point for a child's first complete sentence.

As always, follow your child's lead with this book. If they seem interested – keep going! If not, save some pages for later. The more you read this book with your child, the more familiar they will be with the sentences and verbs. You can pause after the word 'is' to see if they will fill in the verb. Example: The giraffe is…(pause)…eating. Eventually, your child will be able to "read" the book all by themselves if you say, "tell me what they are doing."

Have fun reading!

Cara

Cara Tambellini Danielson M.A. CCC-SLP
instagram.com/caraspeech
caraspeechtherapy.com

Let's see what all of the animals are up to today!

What are they doing?

The giraffe is eating.

The bird is flying.

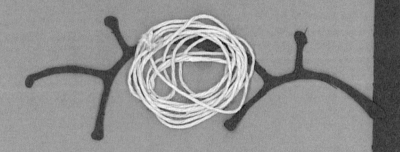

The cheetah is running.

The dog is drinking.

The lion is sitting.

The fish is swimming.

The crab is crawling.

The frog is
hopping.

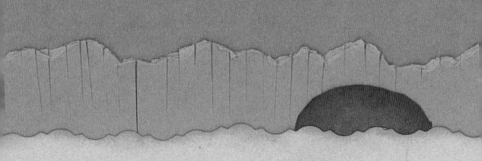

The koala is climbing.

The cow is pooping.

The cat is
sleeping.

The pig is rolling.

The penguin
is sliding.

Made in the USA
Monee, IL
25 April 2022